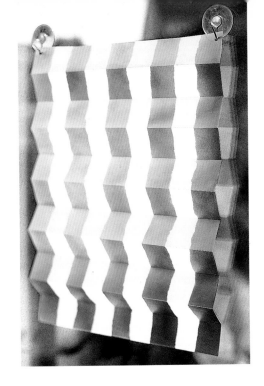

RECIPES & IDEAS

WINDOWS

RECIPES & IDEAS

WINDOWS
Simple Solutions for the Home

by Richard Lowther and Lynne Robinson

CHRONICLE BOOKS
SAN FRANCISCO

First published in the United States in 2000 by Chronicle Books

Editorial Director: Jane O'Shea

Consultant Art Director: Helen Lewis

Project Editor: Nicki Marshall

Consultant Editor: Eleanor Van Zandt

Design Assistant: Jim Smith

Production: Julie Hadingham

Special Photography: Richard Foster

Styling: Wei Tang

Picture Researcher: Nadine Bazar

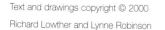

TT390
.L694
2000

Library of Congress Cataloging-in-Publication Data

Lowther, Richard.

Windows: recipes & ideas: simple solutions for the home /
by Richard Lowther and Lynne Robinson

    p.   cm.

ISBN 0-8118-2720-8

1. Draperies. 2. Draperies in interior decoration. 3. Window shades.
I. Robinson, Lynne. II. Title

TT390.L694 2000   99-37296

747'.3—dc21   CIP

Printed and bound in Hong Kong

Interior design and layout by Quadrille Publishing

Cover design by Amy Knapp

Distributed in Canada by Raincoast Books
8680 Cambie Street
Vancouver, British Columbia V6P 6M9

10 9 8 7 6 5 4 3 2 1

Chronicle Books
85 Second Street
San Francisco, California 94105

www.chroniclebooks.com

Note: When following instructions for the projects, check the Practicalities section at the back of the book for a full tool kit of equipment required (page 80). Both standard and metric measurements are given for the projects; use either all standard or all metric as the two are not necessarily interchangeable.

Page 1: A simple, accordion-pleated paper sunshade that will fold away on dull days.

Page 2: A collage of silhouettes hung in a window on the sunny side of the house.

Page 5: Signwriter's paint, stencils, and masking tape are used to create an elegant painted window.

contents

introduction

1. Foursquare and unadorned, this minimalist sculptural window doubles as an observation post for the garden.

2. The frame's structure, borrowing from traditional windows and the garden trellis, throws geometric patterns around the room on sunny days. The windows can be closed off with screens that swing over on arms.

Windows can be a room's biggest asset. They give access to the heat of the sun, protect us from the winter cold, and present a view of the world beyond. Perhaps most importantly, they let in the light in all its variety, be it a natural wash of energizing sunshine, filtered and diffused with translucent fabrics, or light dramatically shaded with blinds, screens, and opaque materials. Without windows, life would be a glum and gloomy affair and our houses bereft of atmosphere.

This book is an unashamedly modern and highly practical approach to window treatments. The creative ideas and projects described here use materials in innovative ways and are in tune with an understated, easy way of living that will reflect and express a spirit of confidence. Contemporary fashion and interiors use materials and concepts interchangeably and share a common ground. Decoration no longer has to be a permanent installation but can change with the mood and season as easily as a pair of shoes.

1. A wonderful four-paned window offers an unobstructed view; privacy is not a concern here.

2. Windows that open on two sides fill the cool, clean room with airy light.

3. These inward-opening arched windows, set in a shallow recess, are elegant left uncurtained.

4. Plain shades will cover any shape; this one satisfies the need for privacy without diminishing the purity of a perfect circle of light.

5. Extending the sill into a table— on both sides of the window— can give a sense of outdoor eating all year round.

6. Medium-sized rectangular windows are often overdressed with valances and draperies, but this simple roller shade screens off the world, filters the light, and is in tune with the graceful simplicity of the room.

The shape

It is very unlikely we will ever be able to choose our "must have" window, placed in the room of our dreams. We must therefore make the best use of what we have, whether a small opening or a whole wall of glass. Many houses have windows typical of a region or a period, such as bays or dormers, which offer their own individual style, but modern houses and extensions may have large windows that slide and swivel open or panes that are raked across the roof.

Whatever their style, some windows will be so handsome you may wish to leave them bare or use only a hanging to enhance their features. If you need to find a solution to the recurring problems of cutting down light, keeping in warmth, or hiding a view, you can choose a shade, blind, or screen that covers only the glass, or paint or etch a design or pattern directly onto the window pane. Delicate translucent fabrics will also give a measure of privacy and will control the light without detracting from the window shape.

Curtains or draperies are often called upon to hide or disguise a small or unattractive window; hanging them wide or long will alter the apparent proportions or size. Alternatively, consider hanging a translucent square or rectangle before the window, which will hide everything but allow a suffused light—to give a silhouette in reverse.

If the window is set into a recess, your options are increased, as it is easier to combine elements of different window treatments—for example, hanging a light, airy fabric inside a heavier, more robust screen for nighttime or combining translucent roller shades with comforting draperies. Such solutions offer a simplicity and clarity that will perfectly complement the style of the room.

If the window is well designed it may not need insulation. But if it does, or you want blackout, a drapery of heavy material need not be the only choice available. A lighter, natural material can be given a backing of blackout lining fabric, which is available in a cream colour.

Windows can be fitted quite low down on a wall, which is useful here, as it illuminates the stairs. Bathed in its glowing light is a collection of umbrellas. Frosted glass louvers control the light levels of another window farther down the stairs.

Reduced to essentials, this totally serene bedroom is lit by a still light, filtered through the simplest of screens.

2

1. Traditional draperies, here reaching the floor to disguise the shape of the window, combine well with contemporary shades.

2. The raw light coming through this wall of windows would be too severe without the multiple small curtains that bedeck it.

3. The arched window retains its handsome presence in the room behind this wall-to-wall, subtly colored voile.

4. A window covering need not be elaborate, as these panels, simply hung over the top of each pane, illustrate.

Another solution is to make shades from a thick opaque material, such as felt; hung from hinged bars, like internal shutters, they will open up stylishly for the day and fold in like wings at night. Consider using internal wooden shutters, which can be cut to fit even arched windows and will easily fold away into a recess. Japanese screens can also be hung as shutters and allow a hazy light to come through. Freestanding screens are an excellent solution for awkward shapes or unusually positioned windows.

Creating the atmosphere

The contemporary home is a fairly informal place with an ambience of relaxation and understated style. This can be achieved whatever the interior scheme or personal taste, from relaxed classic to modern minimalist. When designing a window treatment, remember that the choice of material, the manner in which it is hung, and the way it changes the light all contribute to the atmosphere of each room and the general character of the home.

The mood of a room will be affected hugely by changing light, transparency, translucency, and movement. The raw light that comes streaming in can be blocked, chopped up, or distilled as the mood takes you. Highlights, shadows, and soft patches of suffused light are the basic elements available for creating atmosphere.

The materials with which you clothe your window are vital to the overall look and feel of the design; time spent searching for them and experimenting will be rewarding.

In addition to traditional drapery fabrics, try saris, rugs, or blankets, or fabrics such as suede, knitted wool, or mosquito mesh. They not only will open up new ways to manipulate the light but are materials that will intrigue.

Color in the contemporary interior is generally soft and matte, in keeping with the relaxed ambience. This does not outlaw the brighter vivid colors, however, since these evoke the exotic and, used with care, will brighten an atmosphere without overwhelming the room.

1 Internal shutters that pivot out on arms give opportunities for screening and deflecting light in different ways.

2 Ideal for inward-opening French windows, these simple internal shutters glow translucent when sunlight passes through.

3 These internal shutters are combined with external shutters for greater control over the light and an added measure of security.

Hardware should be chosen to complement the material and not detract from a carefully considered look. Decorative poles and traverse rods may have a place with heavy materials, but the sliding rings and the cords can be too fussy for lighter fabrics and modern windows, which will usually require more delicate loops and slender poles. A tensioned steel cable is unobtrusive, allowing delicate fabrics to float free, unencumbered by a heavy top bar. Such touches will lighten the mood as well as the look of an interior.

Screens offer an alternative to hangings. Placed and manipulated to catch and throw the light in ways draperies cannot, they can be used at night to retain privacy, offering a simple and effective solution for a modern space.

Smaller touches also help to create atmosphere. Stained glass, sign writing, and etching can be mimicked with modern products for a quick and easy transformation. Alternatively, motifs or designs can be stuck to the panes for special occasions or for permanent decoration.

2

recipes and ideas

Shutting out the world satisfies a primal urge, imparting a feeling of security and warmth and signaling the end of the day. Sitting undisturbed in a haven of cozy tranquillity is restorative, allowing time for relaxation and contemplation. Emerging from the comforting retreat of our cocoon, we can then be re-energized during that wonderful moment when we uncover the window and let the morning light flood in.

blacking out

Despite our love of big windows, we still want the option of closing them off altogether. An opaque layer of fabric is not only psychologically comforting; it allows us to go about indoors unobserved and gives us total control over the light. In a cold climate the insulation is also welcome, particularly if the window is of a rickety construction and allows heat to escape. Fortunately most problem windows can be tamed or eliminated, and so designs for window treatments can now be devoted to being effective shields to light.

1 The heavy blackout which wraps up the window at night is lifted to one side during the day to let in light filtered through a translucent shade.

2 The placing of this drapery, together with its vertical folds, perfectly matches the geometry of the room. Here it is being used to control the direction of light by shutting out the daylight from the back of the room while another window floods the table from the side.

1. Two layers of fabric hang over these windows on separate rods, which allows total control over the amount of light in the room: the sheer white curtains give full, filtered light; and when blackout is required, the thicker draperies can be pulled across.

2. Blackout draperies need not be gloomy and dark, as this interior of light, natural coloring shows.

3. Velvet is a popular choice for many, combining warmth and opacity with a touch of grandeur which need not always be retrospective. Modern treatments allow it to dovetail with contemporary interiors.

Blackout will result from the combined effect of the material and the manner in which it is hung. The material need not be dark and heavy, but light can pass through most woven fabrics so if you are using these, you will need to make a backing or a lining of opaque material. Lightweight fabrics can be backed with a blackout lining fabric of rubberized cotton. More flexible solutions can be found by using layers of fabric hung separately or shades combined with curtains or draperies to bring the light down in stages.

Draperies can stylishly black out a contemporary interior if imaginatively chosen and hung. Besides decorator fabrics, other materials can be used; dress your windows in felted wools, moleskin, shantung silk, or Polarfleece—an efficient and lightweight insulative fabric often used to make outdoor clothing. Consider materials used elsewhere in the home, such as blankets, rugs, or bedspreads; these are already associated with comfort and warmth and will carry this message to the window.

The way the curtain or drapery is hung should not be overlooked. Drapery rods were once hidden behind valances or a swag slung in front, but these sometimes look dated in a contemporary home. Conventional traverse rods are unobtrusive and ideal for draw draperies. Stranded steel cable with stainless steel fittings (as used on yachts) is clean and efficient; it is ideal for hanging layers of material, as three or four cables take up little space in a window recess. Stretched rope offers a natural look; or for a fresh approach, adapt a bright climber's rope. Variations on curtain rings include straps, loops, and ties, or eyelets set into the fabric.

An alternative to draperies is a shade of thick material; the fixtures are unobtrusive, and the material can hang flat against the window. The very flatness of a shade is its beauty: it is a contemplative surface, unfussy and unpretentious. If made much larger than the window, it will shut out the light altogether; but if made just a little bigger, it will allow daylight to glow around the edge as dawn breaks.

1. The lining of this drapery, here simply hoisted to let in the light, helps add a layer of blackout as well as insulation.

2. With draperies drawn, you have total control over the lighting and atmosphere in a room. Here the glossy velvet draperies glow in artificial light, adding a warmth and richness to the dining area.

The range of good materials for shades is wide. Flexible fabric can offer warmth and security and can also be rolled up, hoisted, or folded to one side of the window. Stealthily indulgent satin and velvet and sumptuous suede are sleek and add a soft quality to any room. For a more modest, folksy look, seek inspiration in an embroidered blanket or an Amish-style quilt. Canvas, as used in the older style of tent, is simple, offering insulation as well as blackout; but avoid open weaves, which allow some light through.

More unusual materials can be found at the outer extremes of the textile industry: thick felt or neoprene rubber, bought from an industrial supplier, hang flat and square and blend well in most contemporary interiors. Each brings its individual qualities to a room, as felt has a natural softness around the edges whereas the austerity of rubber combines with a hint of decadence. Both can be rolled up, hung from hinged bars, or removed from the window and placed on the wall to have a second role as minimalist art.

Roll-Up Shade

A quiet corner of contemplation using an Eastern-style satin fabric stenciled with an Indian hand print.

fabric—antique gold moiré
sewing machine and thread
wooden batten and hardware
wooden pole
2 metal rods (6 in. [15 cm.] long)
6 screw-in hooks

1 Cut the fabric to size: allow an extra ⅝ in. (1.5 cm.) on each side of the width; and for a handsome thick roll at the bottom of the shade (even when the shade is down), cut the fabric a good third longer than the window.

2 Turn back ⅝ in. (1.5 cm.) of material on each side of the shade, press, and zigzag-stitch in place.

3 Cut the wooden batten and pole to the finished width of the shade.

4 Drill a hole in each end of the wooden pole, and hammer a metal rod into each end.

5 Wrap the top of the fabric around the batten, stapling it to the back.

6 Staple the bottom edge of the shade around the pole.

7 Attach the batten to the wall above the window [see Battens, p. 90].

8 Screw in three pairs of hooks at intervals up each side of the frame to hold the shade at different heights.

Suede Vertical Roman Shade

A sensuous, coffee-and-cream suede shade with an indulgent touch.

4 skins of dress-weight suede
1½ in. x 2 in. (4 cm. x 5 cm.) suede strips
flexible glue
5 wooden dowels
10 large washers
epoxy resin
slim tacks
fine lawn fabric for lining
five 3½ in. (8 cm.) metal pegs
two 2 in. (5 cm.) metal pegs

1 Choose suede skins that, when sewn together, will generously cover the window, with an additional 11½ in. (29 cm.) on the finished width and 4 in. (10 cm.) on the finished height (this includes a ⅝ in. [1.5 cm.] seam allowance).
2 Stitch all four pieces together, with right sides facing, to form a large chessboard.
3 Glue the seams open flat and glue a 1½ in. (4cm) hem at top and bottom.
4 Fold and topstitch five 1 in. (2.5 cm.) rod pockets across the shade—one at each edge, one at the center, and one at each quarter line [see Channels and tucks, pp. 86–7].
5 Cut five ⅝ in.- (1.4 cm.-) diameter dowels ¾ in. (2 cm.) longer than the shade, with lined-up slots cut in each end, and slide them into the pockets. The fit should be snug.
6 Resin-bond a large washer into each slot.

7 Hammer in a slim tack at the top of each rod to secure the suede.

8 Check the hang of the shade, then add tacks in the bottom of the rods.

9 Hide the tacks with suede strips glued around the pockets.

10 Line the shade with fine lawn fabric slipstitched in place.

11 Fix the five long pegs equidistant above the window to hang the shade from, and the two smaller pegs on either side of the sill to hold it in place.

12 To open halfway, shift the first two rods back two places. To open three-quarters, take it off its pegs, turn it to face the window, and hang it on the two pegs, leaving a suede face out.

Denim

A rugged look in denim and rope.

denim fabric
lining material
1½in.- (4cm.-) wide webbing
heavy-duty ocher thread
sturdy eyelets
jute rope
tensioner and hardware

1 Decide on the fullness of the curtain and cut your fabric to size [see Planning allowances for lined draperies and shades, p. 80].

2 Although denim is already fairly light-proof, additional lining will give the curtain extra body [see Lined curtains and draperies, p. 81]. Reinforce the top edge with the webbing.

3 Using heavy-duty thread, outline the curtain with two rows of top-stitching, 1¼ in. (3 cm.) apart, mimicking the look of jeans.

4 Between the rows of stitching along the top edge, mark the position of the eyelets at regular intervals.

5 Cut the hole accurately for each eyelet with scissors, and hammer in the eyelets according to the manufacturer's instructions.

6 Pass the jute rope through the eyelets, then hang the curtain [see Cables and ropes, pp. 88–9].

Note: Tensioners are more usually used with steel cable, but can be used with rope [see pp. 88–9].

Quilt

A Chinese quilt to keep in the warmth.

slub silk fabric
lining material
polyester batting
stranded embroidery floss
1in. (2.5cm) curtain rings
steel pole plus hardware
S-shaped butcher's hooks

1 Cut the silk to size [see Planning allowances for lined draperies and shades, p. 80], adding 1¼in. (3 cm.) all around.

2 Cut the lining and batting to the size of the finished curtain.

3 Assemble the curtain, sandwiching the batting inside and stitching the side seams together, then hand-sewing the top and bottom hems [see Padded lined curtains or draperies, p. 81].

4 Run a line of hand stitches down each side, tiny on the front, longer on the back, and ⅜–¾in. (1–2 cm.) in from the edge to form a padded border.

5 For the mattress quilting, mark out the positions to complement the design of the fabric—around 6 in. (15 cm.) apart. Using six strands of embroidery floss, knot together the layers of the curtain at each mark.

6 Along the top edge, in line with alternate rows of knots, sew on the curtain rings.

7 Fix the steel pole to the frame above the window [see Poles, p. 89].

8 Hang using the butcher's hooks.

Bobble Banket

Wrap up your window in a blanket, with dog collars for curtain rings.

3

fringed blanket

wool lining

tapestry yarn with needle

dog collars

waxed curtain pole plus hardware

1 Find a fringed blanket at least 10% wider than your window, and cut some wool lining ⅜ in. (1 cm.) smaller all around than the blanket.

2 Slipstitch together along the top edge only, just below the fringe, leaving the sides loose and open.

3 Through both thicknesses, cut a row of ¾ in. (2 cm.) slots, 1½ in. (4 cm.) below the fringe and approximately 8 in. (20 cm.) apart.

4 Buttonhole stitch these with tapestry yarn; loop a dog collar through each.

5 Fix the pole above the window [see Poles, p. 89].

6 Fasten dog collars loosely around the rod. The curtain will slide easily back and forth.

Rug

Hanging a thick rug is a quick way to obscure the light and block out the cold.

rug
strong bulldog clips
⅛ in. (4 mm.) stranded steel cable
tensioner and hardware

1 Select a rug that is just a little longer than the window and around twice its width.
2 Thread strong bulldog clips—enough to grip the rug approximately every 9 in. (22 cm.)—along a length of robust ⅛ in. (4 mm.) steel cable.
3 Install the steel cable across the window (see Cables, p. 88).
4 Mark the rug at approximately 9 in. (22 cm.) intervals with chalk or a scrap of masking tape.
5 Suspend the rug from the clips at these markings. The rug should hang like a gently undulating wall.

There is nothing more uplifting than sunlight blasting through a window, but there are times when, left unfettered, daylight creates too harsh a contrast, bleaching out or casting into shadow the details of a room. Natural light may also be too unremitting for a study or living room, where a soft, diffused, or broken light can create the right mood and offer an environment more conducive to working or relaxing.

filtering the light

We can filter as much or as little of the light as we want, letting it enter the room in the softest of washes or chopping it up into geometric patterns which, on sunny days, move across the room as the day progresses. Semi-transparent or translucent materials fixed over a window keep the harshness of the light firmly on the outside, reducing the gleam on shiny surfaces and leaving softly dappled floors, walls, and furniture. Such gentle illumination is an essential element in the relaxed look of a living room or bedroom.

1 A simple floor-to-ceiling screen leaves this minimalist room washed in light, softening the reflections on the modern interior and infusing the room with calm. The world meanwhile stays visible in soft focus.

2 Gaps between these loosely hung gauze curtains reveal a pierced screen which reworks the sun into large droplets of liquid light.

1. Sky-colored transparent shades cut back the glare of the sun without interrupting the splendid panorama beyond.

2. To retain the placid nature of this room, skylights have been simply shaded to filter the light from above, while the fabric shades can be folded up to allow a controlled level of sunlight.

3. A room for rest. The light percolates through simple roller shades, the moon and stars lulling you to sleep and the morning sun gently waking you.

Many fabrics are designed for just this purpose: voile, muslin, and organdy, among others. If you broaden your search you will find fine linens and silks, chiffon, organza, tulle, and other fabrics from the fashion industry. Open-weave interlinings and stiffeners, such as buckram or tarlatan, make interesting alternatives. Metal meshes, translucent plastics, and paper can be put to use also.

These materials cover the whole range, from barely flexible to soft and easily draped. Stiff fabrics hang flat and

can be used for roller shades and fixed screens. Flat shades of a single color look like elegant minimalist paintings which change as the light levels increase and diminish during the day. More transparent materials include the finest micro-fiber and metal mesh, which can be used in layers to produce a moiré effect. For a more natural look, use a coarser open weave, such as tarlatan, with a gently undulating edge.

Simply hanging starched muslin or organdy panels across the window opening is ideal for a bedroom; tie them to pegs set in the wall or onto a slim cane. Their crispness will keep them in good shape, but their lack of weight will allow them to waft about gently when a window is open, adding movement to the repertoire of effects. The light can be manipulated by layering softer, looser fabrics, hanging them in folds or decorating them with pleats and tucks.

Using a neutral, unadorned material will keep the light looking natural and easy. Introduce soft color if you wish your material to play a bigger role in the interior scheme,

or personalize it with subtle motifs sewn or stenciled on the fabric. For a more vibrant look use colors that leap into life as the sun shines through and, even on dull days, cheer up a room. Colored glass, or paint on glass, can be very dramatic, and, used shrewdly, will offer a shimmer of vitality.

Explore the numerous possibilities of contemporary plastic materials. They can perform their traditional role in a bathroom or be used in other rooms for a fun, youthful look. Textured or patterned material also attracts the eye and

offers numerous visual effects as the sunlight touches upon it at different points throughout the day.

If we filter the light coming into a room we cannot help but cut down the view too—from both directions. Semi-transparent material can turn an uninspiring or distracting view into an impressionist painting or render it in the subtle tones of an old engraving seen through tissue paper. If the view is still too unattractive, use layers of fine translucent fabrics to mask it.

Light can also be filtered through slats hung in front of the window. Venetian blinds are very versatile; apart from diffusing the light in a different way, they chop up an unwelcome view into animated strips of color. Matchstick blinds work effectively and offer a more natural ambience for those who find venetian blinds too harsh. Improvise on the same theme with rush or grass mats, removing sections of the mat to let in the light. They are easily hung from bars and can be rolled up when full light is required.

1 The finest of meshes will redraw the view in soft focus while letting the light flow in, casting silhouettes on the screen and light patterns on the floor.

2 A wall-to-wall venetian blind, reminiscent of a cinema screen with ghostly windows projected onto it. Individual treatments on each window would be incompatible with the large shapes and lack of clutter that give this room its character.

1 Whereas blinds manipulate the light primarily in horizontal bands, shutters allow vertical slashes of light to enter a room. The more you have, the better able you are to control the light. Here they are of colored transparent material, Japanese in style.

2 Micro-fiber roller shades attached to individual windows gently filter the light, keep out inquisitive looks, and are a perfect foil for the loose curtains which swing out before them on pivoting battens. This fresh take on net curtains allows for the two elements to be deployed in a variety of ways to suit the mood of the moment.

3 A wall of layered fabric, beyond which the light from the windows gently glows.

For a more contemporary, graphic look, cut and folded paper offers another avenue of ideas. Seek inspiration from lattice and fretwork or the windows of Arabian palaces, an excellent modern example of which is the building of the Institute of the Arab World, Paris. Good-quality paper can be bought in large sizes or on rolls and is easy to cut designs into. This solution looks magnificent as a fixed installation over a large window and effectively hides a poor view or unattractive window.

If access to the window is necessary, attach the paper to light frames, which can be hooked or hinged, shutter-like, to the window frame. Similarly, simple latticework could be woven from parchment-like paper or translucent strips of plastic and hung in the same way. For smaller windows adapt small pieces of fretwork or split cane work to evoke Islamic ornamentation. Experiment with different colors and textures of paper and plastic, either on their own or in combination, as these can offer strikingly individual effects.

Cut-Paper Shade

Cut-paper screens can mask the view and alter the light in exciting, graphic ways, by casting patterns in light and shadow on the floor and walls on sunny days.

white drawing paper (large roll)
blue drawing paper
wooden batten and hardware
aerosol glue
double-sided tape
flat metal bar

1 Cut the paper to size with an X-Acto knife, adding an allowance for wrapping around a bottom bar and a top batten.

2 Plan the position of the four squares of blue paper, and glue in place with aerosol glue.

3 Plan the layout of the triangles in the squares – accuracy is important for the architectural look of this shade.

a) For a 16½ in. (44 cm.) square, begin by marking dots every 1½ in. (4 cm.) along the top, bottom, and right-hand sides of the square [see Cut-paper shade diagram 1, p. 84].

b) Place a ruler vertically on the square, aligned with the first dots in from the right-hand edge. Mark a line of dots starting at ¾ in. (2 cm.) from the top, then every 3 in. (8 cm.) until ¾ in. (2 cm) from the bottom.

c) Align the ruler vertically with the next pair of dots in from the right-hand side and mark another line of dots down the paper, this time at every 1½ in. (4 cm.).

d) Mark the next line of dots as for step b.

e) Mark the fourth line of dots as for step c.

4 Continue in this way across the square.

5 Using an X-Acto knife, cut the two longer diagonal sides of each triangle and score the shorter vertical side [see Cut-paper shade diagram 2,p. 84].

6 Staple the paper to the batten at the top of the shade [see Battens, p. 90].

7 Fold a bottom channel, holding it in place with double-sided tape, and slip in the metal bar.

8 Attach the top batten to the window frame, taking care not to damage the paper [see Battens, p. 90].

Once the shade is hung, you can enjoy the task of opening each triangle and see emerge a drawing in light.

Painted Roller Shade

Sunlight filtered through stiff gauze.

tarlatan fabric

squares of paper

2in.- (5cm.-) wide masking tape

baking parchment

thick white acrylic paint

paint roller

palette knife

flat metal bar

roller from plain roller shade and
  hardware

1 Remove existing shade from roller.

2 Cut the fabric to window length
plus 10 in. (25 cm.).

3 Sew a channel for the bottom bar
[see Channels and tucks, p. 86].

4 Plan a design with squares of paper.

5 Mask around the larger squares
with torn tape [see Masking, p. 96].

6 Remove the squares of paper.

7 Protecting the surface below with
baking parchment, apply thick white
acrylic paint with a roller.

8 Remove the parchment backing
and hang the shade up to dry.

9 Mask the smaller squares as
before, but apply the paint in a
thicker layer with a palette knife.

10 Correct any fabric distortion
when dry, if necessary, using an iron,
a press cloth, and a water spray.

11 Drill a center hole in the metal bar
and slide into the bottom channel.

12 Make and attach the pull
[see Making pulls, p. 85].

13 Attach the fabric to the roller
and hang up the shade, following
the manufacturer's instructions.

Felt Shade

This shade was inspired by the peaceful and serene beauty of Tadao Ando's Church of the Light in Japan.

cotton mosquito netting, buckram,
  or other strong open-weave fabric
¼ in.- (5 mm.-) thick industrial felt
two wooden bars
bolts
hooks and rings

1 Cut the netting to the exact size of your window frame.
2 Using an X-Acto knife, cut the industrial felt into a panel 4 in. (10 cm.) smaller in height and width than the netting. Cut this in half horizontally and vertically to make four equal panels.
3 Lay the net on a flat surface and position the felt panels on top, making sure that the outer edges line up perfectly and that the resulting 4 in.- (10 cm.-) wide cross is both centered and square.
4 Pin in place, then herringbone-stitch the net to the felt all around each panel. The finished work must be completely flat and unwrinkled.
5 Clamp the top edge between the two bars and suspend in front of your window [see Bars with bolts, p. 91].

Transfer this minimalist artwork from the window to the wall when full light is required.

Bungee Shade

This modern, shower-plastic shade springs open when unhooked.

1

shower-curtain plastic
transparent fabric glue
non-ferrous metal rod
wooden batten
electric drill and drill bit
strong round elastic
2 small knobs

1 Cut the plastic to the exact
width required, but allow an
extra 4 in. (10 cm.) on the length.
2 Fold and glue a ¾ in. (2 cm.)
channel at the bottom for a steel rod.
3 Punch three vertical double sets of
holes 1½ in. (4 cm.) apart, starting ¾ in.
(2 cm.) above the bottom edge and
leaving 3 in. (8 cm.) between sets
[see Bungee shade diagram, p. 84].
4 Between these sets of holes,
cut away narrow sections from
the bottom edge—the metal rod
becomes handles in these gaps.

5 Cut the bottom rod and top batten to the width of the shade, and drill holes through both, in line with the holes punched in the shade.

6 Slide in the bottom bar.

7 Wrap the shade's top edge around the batten, stapling it to the back.

8 Cut three equal lengths of strong round elastic. Thread each of them through the batten, down a line of holes, and wind and knot them around the bar, then return up the adjacent line of holes and back through the batten.

9 Adjust the elastic to around half the length of the shade and check that it can be pulled right down before knotting the elastic at the top.

10 Fix the batten above the window [see Battens, p. 90].

11 Screw the two knobs into the window's lower edge to hook the metal bar over when the shade is closed.

Lavender Hazel Branch

*For a fresh look, attach lavender-
scented organdy to a hazel branch.*

organdy (white, ecru, and blue)
narrow satin ribbon
dried heads of lavender
hazel branch with bark removed
hardware

1 Cut each panel of organdy with
a ⅝ in. (1.5 cm.) allowance all around,
keeping enough for the ties.

2 For the 2 in. (5 cm.) border, cut
strips of ecru organdy the width of the
shade by 2 in. (5 cm.), plus ⅝ in. (1.5
cm.) all around. Repeat for the length.

3 Make simple facings all around
[see Making simple facings, p. 82].

4 Stitch pairs of ¾ in.- (2 cm.-) wide
and 8 in.- (20 cm.-) long ties to the
top corners of each panel [see
Making ties for curtains, p. 84].

5 Mark out the position for the lavender bags with chalk, and sew on 6 in.
(15 cm.) lengths of ribbon.

6 Cut the blue organdy into 4 in.
(10 cm.) squares, place a small
amount of lavender onto each,
gather into a bag, and tie onto the
organdy panels.

7 Fix the branch above the window
[see Poles, p89] and tie the organdy
panels to it.

Sheer, Shimmery Fabric On Tensioned Cable

Suspended from wires, these fabrics sparkle with color and life.

3 lengths of transparent fabric
   (2 pink, 1 burnt orange)
⅜ in.- (1 cm-) wide ribbon
dowel
stranded steel cable
tensioner and hardware

1 Leave one of the pink lengths of fabric whole and unadorned; cut two 4 in.- (10 cm.-) wide strips from the other, along the length.

2 On the orange panel, plan out a number of 1¼ in. (3 cm.) horizontal tucks, allowing 2½ in. (6 cm.) for each [see Channels and tucks, pp. 86–7].

3 Hem all side seams.

4 Stitch the tucks in the burnt orange panel.

5 Decorate the trimmed pink panel with vertical appliquéd bands using the material previously cut off [see Appliquéd bands, p. 87].

6 Finish all panels with a ¾ in. (2 cm.) channel at the top and bottom.

7 At the top of each pink panel sew on long double ribbons.

8 Cut lengths of dowel to the width of each panel and slip into the bottom channels.

9 Thread the cable through the top channels and fix in place [see Cables, p. 88].

To vary the look, roll up the panels and tie in place with the ribbon.

Looking out of the window can be a real pleasure, whether to contemplate the garden or seek inspiration, but there are times when opening up a view of the outside world is not an option, either because it is unattractive and uninspiring or because we find other people staring back at us. In these situations, privacy and light can be retained with solutions that will complement the style of the room.

screening the view

Screens hide eyesores and create privacy without radically cutting back the light. Many of the ideas already covered could easily be adapted for this: the paper shade on page 46 makes a superb screen, for example, with or without holes cut into it. Fine voiles and delicate papers act like two-way mirrors—you can see through them only from the darker side, which during the day is usually the room—so no one can look in until the room is lit up in the evening, at which time a less transparent material should be employed.

1 An ideal solution for stargazers: an inverted shade shields those sleeping from outside view while allowing the natural light from the night sky and the sunrise to gently wash over the room.

2 Frosting on bathroom windows offers privacy and natural light; here a small area of the glass is kept clear so that anyone at the sink can gaze out over the trees below.

For a more versatile solution, look for something that can be swung into place or pulled down. Shutters and roller shades do this but have the effect of closing up the room as well as cutting off the view. A reverse roller shade, which covers only the lower half of a window, can cut off a dispiriting view and blinker the roving eye of passers-by but leave you with the daylight and sky views. A more permanent solution is to etch the glass on the lower part of a window, with etching cream, but a similar effect can quickly be achieved by either attaching polyester drafting film (not paper) onto the glass with spray adhesive, or spraying on a coat of frosting varnish. Both of these can easily be removed when required.

Screens need not be in fabric or paper; glassware or thin porcelain bowls on glass window shelves will beguile. A more traditional way of improving the view out is to use plants and flowers. On the inner or outer sill you can plant naturally tall flowers, encourage a climber to grow up a miniature trellis, or try your hand at topiary with box trees.

1 Slatted blinds provide a permanent solution for large windows and will open and close to control the light levels.

2 Individual fabric shades are an unusual solution for a wall of glass and offer a softer, more diffused light.

3 Half shades of pale material provide an effective screen and allow full light into the room.

4 Metal poles will support a veil of fabric tied up like a badminton net, which can double as a room divider and screen.

1. Frosted glass screens off a view effectively but lets in a gentle natural light.

2. Bands of color enliven this bathroom and frame the mountain and sky beyond.

3. Privacy is achieved with a translucent screen which lets natural light from the garden spill into the bathroom.

If you install a planter above the window instead, trailers will cascade down in a living curtain. Choose plants that are leafy all year, such as ivy; in summer you can add trailing lobelias or giant nasturtiums.

A mobile screen, unattached to the window, offers even greater flexibility by hiding the view while allowing the sun to enter and fill the room; set at an angle it will reflect the light back into gloomier corners or create a patch of shade on bright days.

A screen of three panels hinged together can be given a variety of treatments. If it is an open frame construction [see Basic frame construction, p. 92], panels can be made in almost any fabric, from thick canvas to the finest organdy. Other choices include stretched Lycra, rip-stop nylon for a highly colored translucent screen, Japanese paper screens, or panels of pierced or expanded aluminum. Double sheets of toughened glass work well in a frame with pressed flowers or other decorative elements held between them.

Mesh Screen with Pivoting Shades

A visual feast of color and mesh.

metal mosquito mesh
polyester drafting film
invisible tape (if necessary)
fine wire
4 wooden bars (per window)
bolts
open-weave canvas fabric
pivoting bars and hardware
string

1 For each window pane cut two panels of metal mesh to the length of the glass, adding 1½ in. (4 cm.) to the width.
2 Cut a strip of polyester drafting film narrower and shorter than the window (for longer windows, butt-join two pieces with invisible tape).
3 From the film, cut a ladder of slots and punch holes in the corners.
4 Hold the film in place between the mesh by twisting fine wire through the punched holes and into the back panel of mesh.
5 Join the mesh panels together with a double fold ⅝ in. (1.5 cm.) wide down each side. The finished width will be ¾ in. (2 cm.) narrower than the glass.
6 Trap the top and bottom edges of the mesh between two wooden bars. Cut the bars to fit in the frame and bolt together [see Bars with bolts, p. 91].
7 To fix the screen into the window frame, insert small screws sideways into the frame, below the top bar and above the bottom one.

8 For each pivoting screen, cut the canvas to size, with hem/seam allowances.

9 Hem the side seams, and sew ¾ in. (2 cm.) channel hems at the top and bottom [see Channels and tucks, pp. 86–7].

10 Screw the pivoting bars into place above the window and slide the canvas onto them.

11 Make pulls from string and scraps of drafting film tied to the end of each bar [see Making pulls, p. 85].

Bamboo Planter

A living screen of leaves is a gentle, summery way of covering a window.

trailing plants
length of 3½ in.- (9 cm.-) wide
   bamboo
hole cutter (or jigsaw)
potting mixture
gutter brackets

1 Select your trailing plant; the ivy used here lasts all year, is available in many sizes and varieties, and will tolerate shady sites as well as sun.
2 Cut the bamboo longer than the width of the window, making sure that you have a complete section into which the potting mixture will go.
3 Using either a hole cutter or jigsaw, cut three equally spaced 2½ in.- (6 cm.-) diameter holes in each section of the bamboo.
4 Fill the bamboo with potting mixture, insert a plant into each section, and water well.
5 Firmly attach the gutter brackets to the wall above the window and place the bamboo in them.

Note: Regular watering and feeding is made much easier with a funnel and a long-spouted watering can.

Mobile Rubber Screen

A vibrant rubber screen glows
warmly as daylight passes through.

wooden frame and hardware
rubber sheeting
casters
square steel table leg

1 The wooden surround is developed
from our basic frame [see Basic
frame construction, p. 92]. Note that
the top and inner bars are bolted
together to allow you to clamp the
screen in place.
2 Cut the rubber slightly short
in length and punch holes in the
top and bottom, in line with the
bolt holes of the frame.
3 Trap the top edge of the rubber
between the sections of the top bar,
insert the bolts, and tighten them up.
4 Clamp and bolt the bottom edge
of the rubber between the two loose
sections of the inner bar. Pull the
bar down, stretching the rubber,
and bolt in place on the outer frame.
5 Make the base using the same
construction principle as for the frame
[see Wooden cruciform, p. 94].
6 Screw four casters to the underside
of the base.
7 The leg is an inverted square steel
table leg bolted to the frame and
screwed to the base.

Photographic reflectors

A simple sculptural screen using
a striking combination of objects.

glass fiber telescopic fishing pole
cement and coarse sand
child's plastic beach bucket
wooden board and casters (optional)
photographic reflector
small curtain ring
snap-open key ring

1 Make the cement base with the
pole set in it, using the beach bucket
as a mold [see Cement, p. 95].
2 Once complete, the base can either
be placed directly on the floor or, for
ease of movement, set on a wooden
board with casters.
3 Choose your reflector: various sizes
and colors are available. We chose a
light-reflecting combination of silver
on one side and white on the other.
The reflector comes folded up in a
bag and springs open for use.
4 Sew the curtain ring to the fabric
edging of the reflector and the snap-
open key ring to the wire loop at the
top of the fishing pole.
5 Extend the pole to its full height
and clip the reflector in place.

Positioned in front of a window, it will
double as reflector and screen and
will deftly fold away when not wanted.

Windows, with or without fabric coverings, will happily wear an occasional celebratory or seasonal touch, accept a temporary bit of shading, or be the willing site for an imaginative installation, which will bring the window alive and put a smile on people's faces. You can opt to hang designs from the frame, stick things to the window, or even decorate the glass itself as your personal creative touch.

decorative effects

A large variety of materials can be attached to window panes to create innovative effects, from the simplest of paper sunshades to colorful rip-stop nylon kites. Herbs propagated in bags of potting mixtures will make an inventive display when hung from suction cups on the glass; or a collection of objects, such as spectacles or photographs, can be clipped to ribbon stretched across the frame. Glass painting and etching is made easy with modern paints, etch cream, and stencils; for quick stripy abstracts use colored vinyl tape.

1 Curtains, draperies, or shades may not always be appropriate. In such cases the window pane can be painted to create privacy, filter the light, or simply be part of a room's decoration.

2 Etching or frosting on the glass is a simple and effective way of adding an accent to the glass, particularly with etch cream or spray frosting.

Gingham-etched Window

Elegance with stencils and etching.

masking tape

chosen monogram at correct size

transparent film

low-tack spray adhesive

spray frosting varnish (and face
mask) or etch cream

The instructions are for spray varnish. To use
etch cream, follow the package instructions.

1 On the outside pane, starting from
the center, use masking tape to
divide it vertically into equal stripes.

2 Mask a square for the monogram,
lined up precisely with the stripes.

3 Using an X-Acto knife, cut an
equivalent-sized square in transparent
film and cut the monogram stencil into
this [see Stencils, p. 98].

4 Using spray adhesive, attach the
stencil to the inside pane.

5 Starting from the square, divide the
inside pane into horizontal stripes with
the masking tape.

6 Protect the surrounding surfaces
and frame and ensure that the area is
well ventilated. Wearing a face mask,
spray three light coats of varnish onto
both interior and exterior panes,
following the instructions on the can.

7 Once completely dry, remove stencil
and tape; any traces of glue can be
removed later with window cleaner.

Note: If you are using a cellulose-
based varnish, the window can be
washed without causing any damage;
the design can be removed, when
desired, with cellulose thinner.

Leaf Shadows

As light levels rise and fall, the images come and go, even during the evening.

photocopies of leaves, seedheads, and flowers

squares of pastel paper

repositionable spray adhesive

permanent spray adhesive

firm white fabric mesh, cut to size

suction cups with bulldog clips

1 For the silhouettes, attach the photocopies to squares of pastel paper, using repositionable adhesive.

2 With an X-Acto knife, cut around the image through both layers of paper.

3 Peel away the photocopy and permanently glue the cut-out shape to another square of paper. Also glue the shape left behind to another sheet of paper as a negative image.

4 Make enough squares in this way to complete your design.

5 Permanently spray-glue the squares to the mesh in a grid pattern and hang in the window using bulldog clips attached to suction cups.

Light Container

*Glowing lights add a festive feel
at any time of the year.*

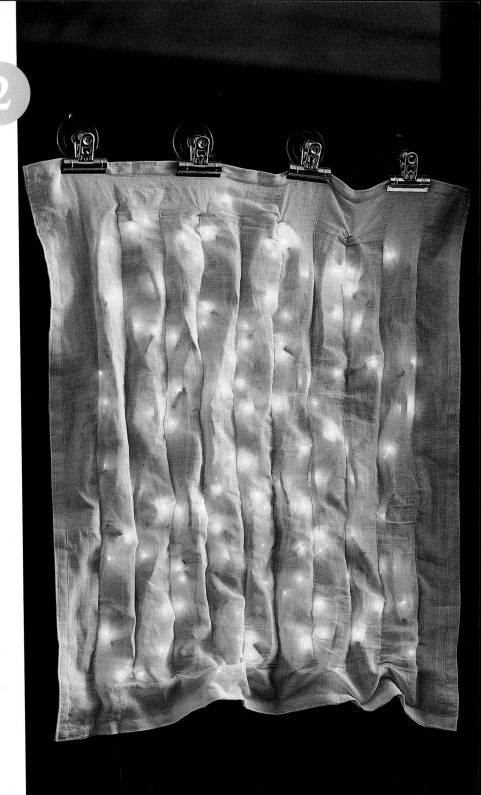

low-wattage string of lights
cream organdy
suction cups with bulldog clips

1 Fold your string of lights in two
and lay it out like a radiator to form
an approximate square in rows
2 in. (5 cm.) apart.

2 Cut two pieces of organdy to
this size, adding 2½ in. (6 cm.)
all around, and press under a ⅜ in.
(1 cm.) hem.

3 Put the two pieces of material
together, enclosing the raw edges,
and stitch vertical lines every 2 in.
(5 cm.), beginning 2 in. (5 cm.) from
the top and stopping 2 in. (5 cm.)
from the bottom. Stitch each line
twice for extra strength.

4 Thread the lights evenly through
the channels, and then double-stitch
the border edge, leaving a small gap
for the cord at the bottom corner.

5 To hang the bag on a window,
clip it to four bulldog clips attached
to suction cups.

6 When ready, plug in, and switch
on the illuminations.

Note: Small, low-power bulbs
are safe to use inside fabric.

Lawn Dress

An angel at your window with a simple lawn dress.

3

fine lawn dress
starch
buttonhole thread
hooked suction cups

1 Starch the dress very stiffly (to collar strength), place it on a hanger, pull it into shape with your fingers, and allow to dry. Do not iron it.

2 Once the dress is dry, attach tabs of masking tape to points of the neck, shoulders, elbows, wrists, hem, and waist, and experiment with its shape and position on the window. To emphasize the silhouette, small tucks can be stitched into the waistband.

3 Once happy with the shape, mark the position of each piece of tape with a pin and remove the dress, leaving the tape on the glass.

4 Sew small button loops at each pin and replace the masking tape on the window with hooked suction cups.

5 Slip the button loops over the hooks, then make your final adjustments.

Note: When the sun is at its height and you require more shade, pull a plain white roller shade down over the dress-decorated window, as here, for a stunning silhouette.

Accordion Shade

An elegant and speedy way to shade a window, using a tough, water-resistant version of tracing paper.

polyester drafting film
wide masking tape
newspaper
metallic spray paint
hooked suction cups

1 For the stripes, mask the film with torn masking tape [see Masking, p. 96], lay it out on plenty of protective newspaper, and spray with the metallic paint, following the manufacturer's instructions.
2 Measure out the accordion pleats.
3 Using the blunt edge of an X-Acto knife, score alternate pleat lines on one side of the film.
4 Turn the film over and score the remainder of the pleat lines.
5 To make the pleats, fold away from the scored edge.
6 Punch a hole in the top corners of the shade to hang it on the glass with hooked suction cups.

3

practicalities

PLANNING AHEAD

This section tells you all you need to know about individual techniques for making the projects. You will have to adapt dimensions to suit your window, which should be carefully measured, especially if you intend to install your design in a recess. The way in which the window is opened should also be taken into account to ascertain which designs are most suitable. At the same time, look at the frame and wall, assessing their suitability to take fixings. Careful planning leaves you free to enjoy making your design and successfully installing it. Assess the design of your curtain or blind before measuring your window: will it hang flat over the window pane, or will it overlap on either side of the frame.

Width: If the installation is to be inside a recess, you should take into account the hardware that will hold it up—rods, cables, and so forth. If the installation is outside a recess, you can, of course, extend it beyond the window according to your needs or the design.

Length: If this is an important element in the design, make sure that you allow for the way in which it is suspended. The length can be adjusted after installation. Note that a cable, pole, or bar will hang below the top of a recess.

Useful Tool Kit You will find the following tool kit handy but check individual projects for particular requirements. These items are not included in the project listings.

Sewing machine	Plastic and metal rulers
Dress pins	Pencils
Needles	Masking tape
Dressmaker's tape measure	Drill and drill bits
Retracting tape measure	Screwdriver
Fabric marking pencil/chalk	Hammer
Iron and ironing board	Saw
Scissors	Staple gun
X-Acto knife/craft knife	Wrench
Hole punch	Pliers

MAKING CURTAINS, DRAPERIES, AND SHADES

Planning quantities for curtains and draperies

Before undertaking any cutting, check, and re-check, your measurements thoroughly: once the original materials have been altered there is little chance of remedy if the measurements are wrong.

The quantity of fabric needed to make a curtain or drapery depends on the fullness wanted. Very full curtains and draperies are less popular in the contemporary home and the tendency is towards those that hang flat or with a gentle movement when closed. Therefore, 1–1.5 times the finished width is probably adequate. Twice the width will give you more movement, whereas 2.5–3 times could look pretty when using very sheer fabric, especially when arranged into pleats or tucks at the top. If your fabric isn't wide enough, join widths together. The finished curtain or drapery should overlap the window by at least 4 in. (10 cm.).

Planning quantities for shades

Allow extra fabric for wrapping around or attaching to fixings, such as a top batten or roller blind pole. In a recess leave a clearance on either side. A blind hung outside a recess is cut to overlap the opening.

Planning allowances for lined draperies and shades

For a lined drapery the lining is cut smaller than the main fabric. As a general rule, 2 in. (5 cm.) is added to each side of the finished drapery and 2 in. (5 cm.) is subtracted from the lining. Then add a ⅝ in. (1.5 cm.) seam allowance to these widths. Add 2½ in. (6 cm.) to the drapery for a top and bottom hem allowance, but add nothing to the lining.

Lined draperies

1 Cut main fabric and lining following the previous instructions. Finish the top and bottom edges of the main fabric with overlock or zigzag stitching. Turn up 1¼ in. (3 cm.) on the lining in either a single or double hem, depending on fabric bulk. Place the lining on the main fabric with right sides facing and edges matching, with the lining 2½ in. (6 cm.) down from the top of the main fabric. Join the ⅝ in. (1.5 cm.) side seams, finishing just above the lining hem.

2½ in.

lining wrong side

2 Turn right side out. Press the lining hem flat, then press the side seams to give a 2 in. (5 cm.) hem at each edge.

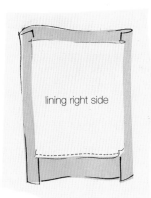

lining right side

3 Press the top hem over the lining, mitering the corners. Slipstitch in place.

miter the corner

lining

slipstitch in place

For a very neat finish, turn under a ⅜ in. (1 cm.) hem first, then the rest of the hem allowance, and slipstitch as above.

4 Press up the bottom hem, mitering the corners, and slipstitch in place. Sew the loose bottom corners of lining in place over the hem with a few stitches.

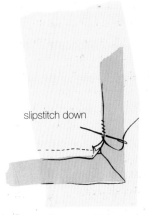

slipstitch down

Padded lined curtains or draperies

For a padded curtain or drapery, cut the lining and batting to the exact finished size. Add just 1¼ in. (3 cm.) all around on the main fabric. Placing the lining and batting 1¼ in. (3 cm.) down from the top of the fabric, stitch ⅝ in. (1.5 cm.) side seams as before. Turn right side out and press to form a ⅝ in. (1.5 cm.) facing on each side. Turn a ⅝ in. (1.5 cm.) double hem at top and bottom, mitering the corners, and slipstitch in place.

Simple facings for shades, curtains, and draperies

1 Cut the main fabric piece to the finished size plus ⅝ in. (1.5 cm.) all around. For a 3 in. (8 cm.) facing, cut two strips the width of the panel plus 1¼ in. (3 cm.) by 4¼ in. (11 cm.). Repeat for the length.

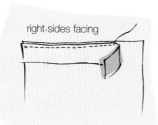

right sides facing

2 Put the wrong side of the blind to the right side of the facing and join the top edges together. Press under ⅝ in. (1.5 cm.) on the free edge of each facing, then press the facing to the front of the panel and pin flat.

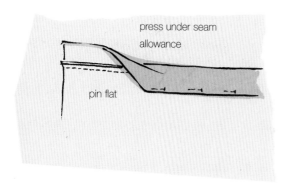

press under seam allowance

pin flat

3 Repeat for the side edges, also pressing under the seam allowances at top and bottom of the facing.

press under seam allowance

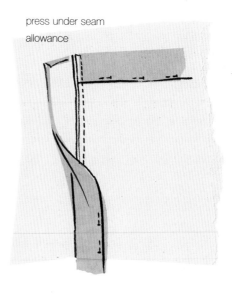

4 Topstitch the facing in place.

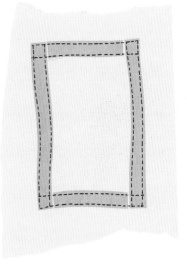

Double facings for shades

1 Cut the shade to its exact finished size. For a 3¼ in. (8 cm.) facing, cut two strips equal to the width of the shade by 6½ in. (16 cm.) plus a ⅝ in. (1.5 cm.) seam

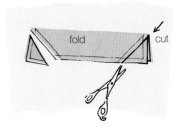

allowance all around. Repeat for the length. To miter the corners, fold each strip in half lengthwise and (using a right-angled triangle) mark the diagonal within the seam allowance. Allow a ⅝ in. (1.5 cm.) seam allowance on the diagonal before cutting.

2 Unfold and join these four strips together along the miters to make the facing, taking the stitching just to the edge of the seamline.

3 Trim excess around the points. Turn right side out and press carefully, pushing the corners out with pointed scissors.

4 Press under seam allowances. Lay the main panel on a flat surface, and sandwich it between the two layers of facing. It must all lie very flat. Pin, then baste carefully through all thicknesses.

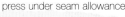
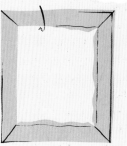

5 Depending on your confidence and sewing abilities, either topstitch through all thicknesses or slipstitch down on both sides.

topstitch

slipstitch

Making shades

Bungee shade diagram

● Punch three vertical, double sets of holes 1¼ in. (4 cm.) apart, starting ¾ in. (2 cm.) above the bottom edge and leaving 3 in. (8 cm.) between holes.

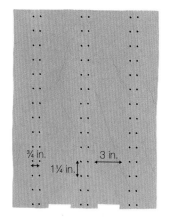

¾ in.   3 in.
1¼ in.

Cut-paper shade diagram

① Measurements are for a 16½ in. (44 cm.) square. Mark dots every 1½ in. (4 cm.) along the top, bottom and right-hand sides of the square. Place a ruler vertically on the first dots in from the right-hand side and mark a dot at ¾ in. (2 cm.), then every 3 in. (8 cm.) until ¾ in. (2 cm.) from the bottom. Mark the next line of dots every 1½ in. (4 cm.), and the third at 3 in. (8 cm.).

② The completed pattern of dots shows the position of the triangles. Cut the two longer, diagonal sides of each triangle, and score the shorter, vertical side.

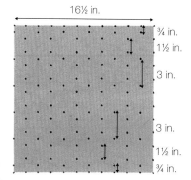

16½ in.

¾ in.
1½ in.
3 in.

3 in.

1½ in.
¾ in.

— cutting line   --- scoring line

Making ties for curtains

① For each separate tie, cut strips of fabric to the required length by twice the width, plus a ⅝ in. (1.5 cm.) seam allowance all around. Fold in seam allowances on both sides and one end.

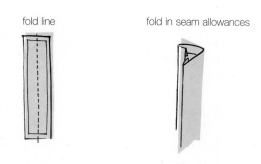

fold line   fold in seam allowances

② Fold the strip in two lengthwise, wrong sides facing, and topstitch up one side, across the top, and down the other side. Fold under the raw edges and topstitch in pairs either side of the top edge of the curtain.

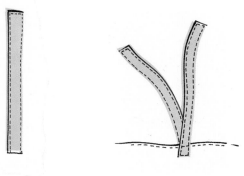

topstitch together   topstitch to top edge of curtain

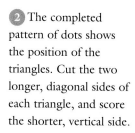

Making pulls for shades and hinged panels

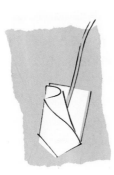

● Any strong and fairly flexible materials, such as artists' primed canvas, polyester drafting film, leather, or suede, is ideal for making pulls. Glue two layers of your material together with a length of cord or string sandwiched between.

● If using this method, it may be advisable to bar-tack just over the cord for extra strength, or topstitch around the pull.

bar-tack

topstitch

● Alternatively, glue the layers together, punch a hole, and thread cord or string through, binding it tightly with fine wire or thread.

Attaching pulls to shades and hinged panels

1 Drill a hole in the center of the bottom batten.

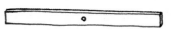

2 Push it into the hem channel and make a corresponding hole in the fabric.

3 Push the cord of the pull through from front to back and secure with a knot.

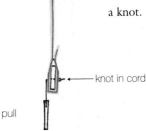

knot in cord

pull

cross section

Channels and tucks

Allow twice the folded depth for each channel or tuck, plus a seam allowance if it falls at the edge of the panel.

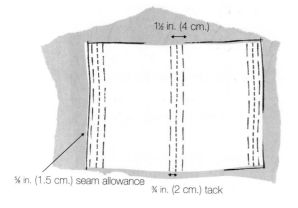

1½ in. (4 cm.)

⅝ in. (1.5 cm.) seam allowance

¾ in. (2 cm.) tack

For a channel that falls on the edge of an unlined panel, press under the seam allowance, fold the channel, and topstitch it in place. Use this same method for creating a hem channel into which a batten, rod or bar is inserted.

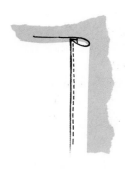

For simple tucks down the length or across the width of a panel, simply mark their positions and fold, wrong sides together. Pin, then topstitch in place.

fold and pin

topstitch

For a lined panel, fold the channel and stitch along the seamline. The raw edge will be enclosed in the lining.

raw edge

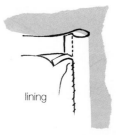

lining

For plastic and suede, glue the seam allowance flat. For suede, stitch along the seamline for extra strength— do not stitch plastic as it could tear along the perforations.

For all open-ended channels, sew the hems before making the tuck.

open-ended tucks

For closed channels, hem after making the tuck.

closed tucks

Appliquéd bands

1 For appliquéd bands running the length of a panel, cut strips to the same length required but add ¾ in. (2 cm.) to the required width. Press under ⅜ in. (1 cm.) down each side of the band.

2 Pin in place on the curtain or shade and topstitch flat.

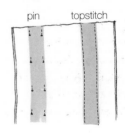

pin   topstitch

HANGING CURTAINS, DRAPERIES, AND SHADES

Cables

Stranded steel cables have to be stretched taut to work. Kits for lightweight curtains are available, but you can make up your own system with elements bought in hardware stores or marine supply stores.

● Equipment needed: two hooks, a cable, two cable grips, and a tensioner. Tensioners for yacht rigging are smart, but expensive; cheaper versions are available for fencing. Good cable grips can be made from electrical connectors stripped of their plastic.

cable grips

tensioner

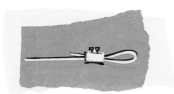

● Make up a piece of cable with loops at each end which, together with the tensioner, will fit loosely between the two hooks screwed into either side of the window. Turn the tensioner and the cable will become taut.

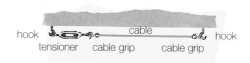

hook   tensioner   cable grip   cable   cable grip   hook

● If the window is narrow and the tensioner is in the way of the curtain, use a third hook screwed lower down the frame, and position the tensioner vertically, out of the way.

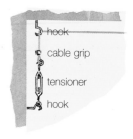

hook
cable grip
tensioner
hook

● For layers of curtains, pass the cable back and forth across the window between sets of hooks before connecting up to the tensioner.

hooks   tensioner

Ropes

A tensioner can also be used to keep ropes taut. Loop each end of the rope over and bind in place with cord. The loop will be too big for the tensioner's hook, so make a link between them with a key ring.

Two different pole holders for use in a recess.

Poles

These are usually wood or metal, as they need to be smooth and stiff. If using a branch, strip off the bark with a knife to reveal the smooth wood underneath. Hardware stores stock a wide range of pole holders which can be attached to the wall or ceiling.

A pole holder for attaching to the wall or ceiling.

A pole holder for a hidden fixing.

Battens

As a top bar for a shade or screen
Fabric or paper can be glued or stapled around a wooden batten of approximately ¾ in. x 1 in. (2 cm. x 2.5 cm.), which is then suspended from the top window frame in one of the following ways:

● Insert three or more L-shaped hooks into the window frame. The number will depend on the width of the window and the weight of the fabric. Before attaching the shade, put the batten in place and mark the position of the hooks. Drill holes of the same diameter as the hooks upward into the batten deep enough for them to slip onto the hooks.

● If you can buy or cut a batten to the same dimensions as a curtain rail clamp, you can use these to hold the top bar. They can be screwed into the wall, frame, or ceiling.

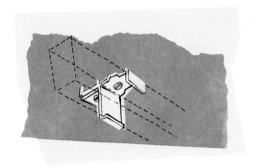

● Screw rings into the top of the batten, and hang it from hooks in the frame or ceiling.

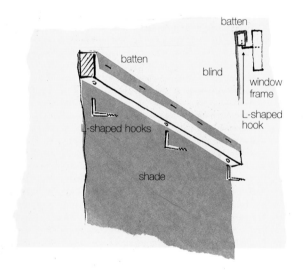

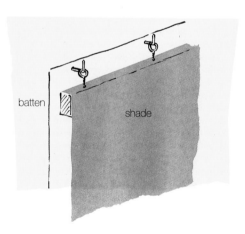

As stiffeners in a channel at the bottom of a shade

● A thin wooden or aluminum strip slotted into a channel will stiffen the bottom of a shade or screen. Heavier metal ones will pull a shade down straight and taut. If round battens are used, shades can easily be rolled up around them.

Bars with bolts

Some materials or designs are not suited to being wrapped around a batten but are better clamped between two lengths of wood.

① Cut two pieces of wood to the same width as the material and to a dimension suited to the overall size of the shade or screen. Through both pieces of wood, drill a series of holes ¼ in. (6 mm.) in diameter (or less for a smaller shade). Space them every 6–8 in. (15–20 cm.), making sure that there is a hole close to each end of the bar.

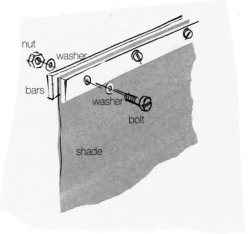

② Place one of the bars in position on the material to be gripped and mark where the holes are. Make a matching set of slightly larger holes in the material. Place the two bars either side of the material and pass ¼ in. (5 mm.) bolts with washers through all three pieces. Place washers and nuts on the other side and tighten with a wrench. The shade can be hung using any of the methods on page 90.

SCREENS AND SHUTTERS

Basic frame construction

Material can be stretched over frames to create simple internal shutters or screens. Making the frames need not involve cutting joints if you can arrange for a woodyard to cut the timber to precise lengths.

1 For each side of the frame you will need two pieces of wood. Cut one shorter than the other by twice the width of the wood. Glue the shorter piece of wood to the centre of the longer piece, to form a corner half lap joint on each end.

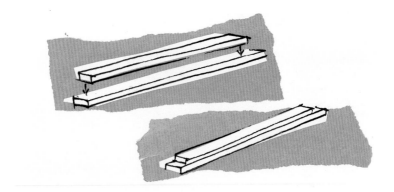

2 Make three more sides in exactly the same way. Sand each side down before assembling your frame. Glue and clamp the joints together, reinforcing them with screws or dowels if you feel the need.

For the screen on page 67 we added a second bar low down inside the frame using the same construction technique. It should be noted that we did not glue this bar together nor the top bar of the frame but bolted them instead, which allowed us to clamp the rubber between them as explained in Bars with bolts, page 91.

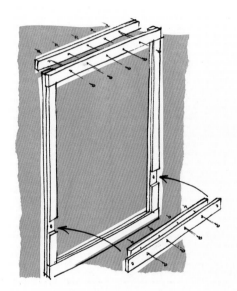

Attaching material to a basic frame

Pull fabric or paper taut, and tack or glue onto one or both sides of the frame. If necessary, glue a trim of tape, a strip of paper or a slim batten onto the join to hide the raw edges. For extra strength, nail on a batten.

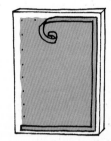

Alternatively, place eyelets in the corners of the fabric and lash to the screen with thonging or cord. Or you could simply pass a loop of strong, round elastic through each eyelet and fasten around a small knob on either side of the frame. Metal mesh and other stiff materials, such as illustration card and plastic, can be stapled or nailed on, or decoratively attached using mirror fixing screws. Hide staples or nails with a trim as above.

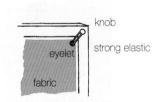

knob
strong elastic
eyelet
fabric

Bases for screens

Wooden cruciform
This uses the same construction principal as the frame.

1 From 2½ in. x 1 in. (6 cm. x 2.5 cm.) timber cut two pieces 25½ in. (65 cm.) long and four pieces 11½ in. (29.5 cm.) long. Glue and screw the smaller pieces along the length of the larger pieces leaving a 2½ in. (6 cm.) gap at the center.

2 When set, sand the two elements, then glue and screw them together to form a cross.

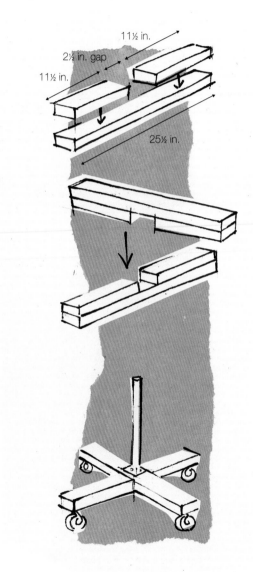

11½ in.
2½ in. gap
11½ in.
25½ in.

3 Stain, wax or paint the cross and then screw a caster below the end of each arm. For an upright to hold your screen, screw in a square steel table leg at the centre of the cross.

Cement

1 First find a mold: a child's plastic bucket is ideal as cement will not stick to it and the sloping sides will not grip the cast when it is set. Alternatives include plant pots, rolls of plastic, or linoleum. The upright pole that supports the screen is placed in the mold before adding the cement which, once hard, will grip it firmly. For a neat finish—and a more stable shape when using a bucket—push the pole through a hole cut in the bottom and balance the bucket between two stools so that the pole hangs down between them.

2 To three parts of coarse sand add one part cement (white Portland cement with pale sand for a stony looking finish, grey Portland for an industrial look). To this add just enough water to make a "dry" mix—too much water will result in a weak cast.

3 Fill the mold in small dollops of cement, tapping each one down with a small bit of wood to ensure that no air holes or cavities are left, particularly on the side of the mold, which would spoil the look of the base.

4 Once the bucket is full, level it off with a trowel and leave to set. Cement must not be allowed to dry out while it is curing, so wrap it in wet rags or plastic film for at least 24 hours before removing the mold.

5 Once it is fully set, you can attach the screen to the pole [see Photographic Reflectors project, pp. 68–9.] Refinements include gluing felt to the base to protect wooden floors or placing it on a block of wood to which casters have been added.

bucket filled with cement

pole pushed through bucket

DECORATIVE TECHNIQUES

Masking

Masking tape is most commonly used to mask off the glass when painting the window frame; it is also indispensable when used in conjunction with spray paint or frosting varnish to create sharp-edged, evenly-spaced stripes. Ordinary transparent tape should not be left on the window for too long, particularly in bright sunshine, as it becomes difficult to remove. A range of specialist tapes are now available which are not too sticky and which can also be used on fabrics, paper, and freshly painted surfaces.

● Attach masking tape to the window to create evenly-spaced stripes, before applying paint or frosting varnish.

● For a less precise edge, buy 2 in.- (5 cm.-) wide tape and tear down its length. For wobbly edges on both sides, it is easier to use two overlapping lengths. An alternative is to use paper—till roll for example—torn and held in place with low-tack adhesive.

torn masking tape stripes

Spray painting

If using spray paint or frosting varnish take care that all areas to be left unpainted are covered in tape or newspaper, including the table, floor and walls. Ideally, work with a face-mask in a well-ventilated room or in the open air. When the design is complete, leave the masking tape in place until the paint or frosting varnish is completely dry to avoid damaging freshly-painted areas.

Painting with a roller

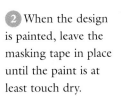 Artists' acrylic paint can be used on fabric. It is best applied with a small, short-haired paint roller. Spread the paint in an even film on a tile to remove excess before applying paint to the fabric.

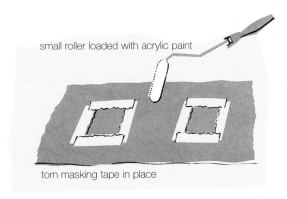

small roller loaded with acrylic paint

torn masking tape in place

2 When the design is painted, leave the masking tape in place until the paint is at least touch dry.

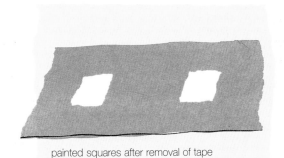

painted squares after removal of tape

Stenciling

For complex shapes you will need a stencil, cut with an X-Acto or craft knife from cardboard, paper or plastic. For single use, ordinary paper will do. For multiple use, choose oiled manila stencil paper or transparent photocopier film.

1 If you have access to a photocopier, you will be able to enlarge or reduce an image to the size you want. If you are unable to use a photocopier, trace the image onto tracing paper. Stick the tracing or photocopy to the stencil paper with low-tack spray adhesive. If using transparent film, photocopy the image directly onto it or trace the image using a marker.

2 Place the stencil paper or film on a cutting mat or sheet of thick cardboard. Using a very sharp knife cut around the edge of the shape. Note that you will be cutting through both photocopy/tracing and stencil paper.

3 Afterward, peel away the photocopy and discard it. A stencil cut from stencil paper can be used as a decorative element itself—place it on a window or screen and let the light take the place of paint.

Painting with stencils on glass

Use low-tack spray adhesive to attach the stencil to the glass. Any adhesive which remains on the window can be removed the next day with window cleaner.

If using spray paint or frosting varnish, the same safety procedures should be followed as for painting with masks. Oil-based paint for glass is best applied with a fine textured sponge snipped to size with scissors. Dip the sponge into the paint and dab onto a tile to remove any excess before stenciling your motif.

1 To produce a stenciled window such as the one on page 5, load an old, bristly decorator's brush with ink, and splay it out firmly on a sheet of paper, pushing it forward slightly a couple of times to create a soft fuzzy flower head; continue until there are six or more flowers with which you are happy. Cut them out and make a flower arrangement to fit your window.

2 Once happy with the design, transfer it to a sheet of cardboard or stencil paper and cut it out using an X-Acto knife.

3 Attach the stencil to the inside of the window using low-tack spray adhesive, and create the design using signwriter's paint and a sponge.

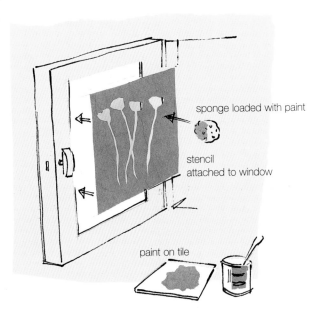

sponge loaded with paint

stencil
attached to window

paint on tile

Suppliers

Ballard Designs
(800) 367-2775
Call for distributors.
- *Window hardware*

Blome
Secaucus, New Jersey
(800) 875-0042
- *Window hardware*

Britex Fabrics
San Francisco, California
(415) 392-2910
- *Wide selection of fabrics,
  sewing supplies*

Crate & Barrel
(800) 606-6387
www.crateandbarrel.com
Call for catalog
and store locations.
- *Curtains, fixtures*

Designer Fabric Outlet
Toronto, Ontario
(416) 531-2810
- *Wide selection
  of discount fabrics*

Drummond Window
Toronto, Ontario
(800) 260-5327
- *Hardware*

Elite Window Fashions
Concord, Ontario
(800) 387-3566
- *Curtains, shades*

F. Schumacher & Co.
(800) 556-0040
Call for nearest distributor.
- *Decorative trimming*

Home Depot
(800) 430-3376
www.homedepot.com
Call for store locations.
- *Shades cut to size*

Homespun
(800) 251-0858
- *Extra-wide fabrics*

Houles-USA
Los Angeles, California
(310) 652-6171
- *Decorative hardware*

Hunter Douglas
Broomfield, Colorado
(800) 438-3883
Call for distributors.
- *Blinds, shades*

Ikea
(800) 959-3349
www.ikea.com
Call for store locations.
- *Shutters, shades and curtains*

Joanne Fabrics
Mississauga, Ontario
(800) 268-2050
- *Wide selection of fabrics,
  sewing supplies*

**Jo-Ann Fabrics
and Crafts**
Hudson, OH
(330) 656-2600
- *Fabrics and
  craft supplies*

Kestral Manufacturing
(800) 494-4321
Call for distributors.
- *Wood shutters*

Kirsch Co.
Sturges, Michigan
(800) 528-1407
Call for distributors.
• *Shades, hardware*

Orchard Supply Hardware
(800) SHOP-OSH
www.osh.com
Call for store locations.
• *Hardware, paints*

Laura Ashley Home
(800) 429-7678
Call for store locations.
• *Country fabrics*

Levolor
High Point, North Carolina
(910) 812-8181
Call for distributors.
• *Metal and wooden blinds*

Michael's
(800) MICHAELS
www.michaels.com
Call for store locations.
• *Craft supplies*

Outwater Plastics Industries
Wood Ridge, New Jersey
(800) 631-8375
• *Film overlay for windows*

Plantation Shutters
Phoenix, Arizona
(602) 272-8291
• *Shutters*

Pottery Barn
(800) 659-5507
www.potterybarn.com
Call for store locations.
• *Curtains, drapes*

Renovator's Supply
Conway, New Hampshire
(800) 659-2211
• *Decorative hardware*

Restoration Hardware
(800) 762-1005
www.restorationhardware.com
• *Decorative hardware, curtains*

Sears
(800) 972-4687
www.sears.com
Call for store locations.
• *Curtains, hardware, paint*

Shade-O-Matic
Downsview, Ontario
(800) 387-2870
• *Shades*

Shutters, Inc.
Chatsworth, California
(818) 882-2235
• *Shutters*

Sunrise Wood Blinds
(800) 818-0059
Call for distributors.
• *Blinds*

The Silk Trading Co.
Los Angeles, California
(213) 954-9290
• *Luxury fabrics,*
  custom draperies

Windoware
Corona, California
(800) 248-8888
• *Blinds and shades*

Index

Authors' acknowledgments

A book of this nature always involves many people with their individual skills and we would like to say thank you to you all. Amongst those who helped us for free are Diane Crawford, whose knowledge and enthusiasm for fabrics was inspirational, and Laure and François Dudouit, who cheerfully let us into their home and whose windows now grace many of our projects. Thank you also to Etiye Dimma-Poulsen of the Galerie Hamelin, Honfleur, whose graceful sculptures stand before our felt blind on page 50. The bobble rug on page 36 is a Musket & Mazullo design. They can be contacted at 242 Saint Pauls Road, Islington, London N1 2LJ; tel: 020 7354 5976.

Publisher's acknowledgments

The publisher would like to thank Caroline Arber for her photography on pages 34–37. Many thanks also to all those who gave permission for their photographs to be included in this book: 1-2 Richard Foster; 6 Marie Claire Maison/ Ingalill Snitt/Catherine Ardouin; 8 Dominique Vorillon/Daly Genik Architects; 9 Undine Pröhl/designer Ricardo Regazzoni; 10 Houses & Interiors/Verne; 11 above left Alexander van Berge/Elle Wonen; 11 above right The Interior Archive/Fritz von der Schulenburg; 11 below left Agence Top/Christian Sarramon; 11 below centre Undine Pröhl/Architect Ron Goldman; 11 below right Richard Glover/Architect John Pawson; 12 Lanny Provo; 12-13 Arcaid/Richard Glover/ Architect John Pawson; 14 left Ray Main/Mainstream; 14 right Agence Top /Pascal Chevalier/Christian Benais; 15 left Camera Press /Raben/Für Sie; 15 right Marie Claire Maison/Gilles de Chabaneix/Catherine Ardouin/designer Jacqueline Morabito; 16 Arcaid/Richard Bryant/Architect Gary Cunningham; 17 left Marie Claire Maison/Nicolas Tosni/ Julie Borgeaud; 17 right Marie Claire Maison/Nicolas Tosni/ Julie Borgeaud; 18 Dominique Vorillon/Architect Jesse Bornstein; 19 Undine Pröhl/Architect Preston Phillips; 20 Richard Foster; 22 Houses & Interiors/Jake Fitzjones; 23 Paul Ryan/International Interiors/designer Bernardo Urquita; 24 Houses & Interiors/Verne; 25 left Maison Madame Figaro/ Ivan Terestchencko/designer Agnès Colmar; 25 right World of Interiors/Chris Kramer; 26 Elizabeth Whiting & Tom Leighton/ designer Charles Rutherfoord; 27 Ray Main/Mainstream/designer Kelly Hoppen; 28-29 Richard Foster; 30-33 Richard Foster; 34-37 Caroline Arber; 38 Arcaid/Richard Bryant/Architect Claudio Silvestrin; 39 Ivan Terestchenko; 40 Dominique Vorillon; 41 left Inside/Maison Française/J L Scotto; 41 right Ray Main/ Mainstream/designer Nick Allen; 42 Deidi von Schaewen; 42-43 Richard Glover/Architect Ben Mather; 44 left The Interior Archive/Henry Wilson/designer Charles Rutherfoord; 44 right Marie Claire Maison/Nicolas Tosni/Josée Postic; 45 Paul Ryan/ International Interiors/designers Kathy Moskal & Ken Foreman; 46-57 Richard Foster; 58 Richard Davies/Architect Future Systems; 59 Paul Ryan/International Interiors/Kastrup & Sjunnesson; 60 Deidi von Schaewen; 61 above Henry Bourne/ Architect Vincent van Duysen; 61 below Paul Ryan/International Interiors/designer Michael Asplund; 62 Houses & Interiors/ Verne; 63 left Undine Pröhl/Architect Wendell Burnette; 63 right Undine Pröhl/ Architect Wallace Cunningham; 64-69 Richard Foster; 70 Ray Main/Mainstream/Mace/Amersham; 71 Ray Main/Mainstream; 72-77 Richard Foster.

BAKER & TAYLOR